TV News Writing Made Easy for Newcomers

STEP-BY-STEP TIPS, TOOLS AND TECHNIQUES TO USE, AND CRUCIAL TRAPS TO AVOID, IN CONSTRUCTING A TV NEWS STORY

TV News Writing Made Easy for Newcomers

Ravi M. Khanna

W V P D

Wisdom Village Publications Pvt Ltd

Knowledge is information. Wisdom is transformation.

A Wisdom Village Publications Presentation
Books from Wisdom Village Publications Pvt. Ltd envision to enhance and enrich their readers with life changing experiences from the business, mind, body and soul genres. They strive towards holistic development.

Editorial Coordinator Anu Anand

ISBN 9789380710174

Published in 2011 by:

W V P D **Wisdom Village Publications Pvt Ltd**
Knowledge is information. Wisdom is transformation.

Wisdom Village Publications Pvt. Ltd
649, O4U, Udyog Vihar, Phase V, Gurgaon, Haryana 122001
www.wvpd.in

To Book Your Orders:
Email: wvpdindia@gmail.com
Or Call: +91 9810800469

Published by Anu Anand for Wisdom Village Publications Pvt Ltd;
Cover Design by Sunil Mathur; Page Setting by Sunil Mathur;
Printed by J.K. Offset Graphics (P) ltd, B-278, O.I.A, Phase-1, New Delhi-20.

Dedicated to my

son and daughter,

Brittan and Samiha,

who often ask me what made me such a good story-teller, not realizing that during my long journalistic journey, all I was doing was telling stories.

CONTENTS

FOREWORD

As I say on the cover, this is not an academic book of theories about writing news. This book is the gist of simple hands-on tools and practical techniques I gathered during the 24 years of my journalistic journey in which I equally delved into writing news for Print, Radio, TV and the WEB in India and overseas.

I learnt these techniques as I changed my career from an "auditor" to "editor". Yes, you read it right. I was a Chartered Accountant by profession before I switched to full time journalism. Although I was the editor of my college magazine, had published articles in English and Hindi, and had worked part-time for AIR and Doordarshan, I was never a full time journalist until I joined Voice of America in Washington. And as I plunged into my new career, I gathered some precious nuggets, which I want to share with you because I feel the newcomers today are facing the same difficulties that I had to overcome the hard way.

As I was thinking about all this, I saw a huge growth in the media industry in India at a very rapid rate and a huge surge in the number of college graduates who were hired by ever growing TV channels. As we see every day, they are doing a very good job, and in some cases, a brilliant job, except when we see them openly editorializing and blatantly inserting their own opinions without any veracity or verification. Although there has been a mushroom growth of private institutions teaching journalism, there still is a need, it seems, to teach our budding journalists about the value of correct, factual and balanced news and the pitfalls of tainting news with opinions.

Sometimes, it seems that the rapidly hired new graduates were either put in front of the camera or behind it with an urgent mission of gathering, digesting, writing and presenting the News and in some cases with very little training. This was a huge responsibility on them. Apparently, some rose to the occasion and others can be seen as just limping along. Obviously, there is cut-throat competition among the channels, and some of them have had no time to think about the "quality" of writing and presenting the news.

So all I have done in this book is to highlight the

traps our newcomers can fall into and techniques to avoid them. Ideally, I want to open an Institute of Journalism in New Delhi and make it affiliated with an American University where I have been on the Curriculum Advisory Board. The idea is that anyone getting a degree from this institute could get admission in this American University for higher studies and specialization. We can also have some top American experts as visiting professors. But then I found out that raising money for this kind of an institute could prove to be an uphill task and could take a long time.

So I felt that as the efforts for the institute continue, this small hand book, on the pattern of Cliff's Notes for students, could be the best way for an old-timer to help the newcomers in appreciating that news should always be balanced, factual, unbiased and correct. Also to make them realize that today there are so many different avenues to get News that if the customers find it tainted, biased or opinionated, they can easily switch to some other channel.

So here is my humble offering in which I am trying to share with you my hard earned experiences on how to construct a news story, for Print, TV, Radio and the WEB.

In the end I must express my genuine gratitude to the wire agencies such as REUTERS, AP, AFP, PTI, UNI and VOA NEWS. I have read and used their stories all my life, and was surely inspired by them when I constructed news examples and exercises for my reader-students.

WARNING AND DISCLAIMER

All news stories included
in this book for students
as examples and exercises
are only fictional and not real.

CHAPTER-1

WHAT IS NEWS?

What is news? It is an account written by you of what happened that is so important that it has to be told to the people in general through newspaper, radio, TV or now on the WEB.

So how to write news really means how to tell a 'story', in our case a 'news story'. You must understand at the very outset that every news item is a story of What happened or What was done or What was said. There are four more "W's", but we will get to that later, in a new chapter.

So all we have to do is to tell it to the listener or viewer (I am going to call them customers from now on) in a way that is easy to understand and interesting at the same time. You have to remember these stories are NOT FICTIONAL BUT REAL STORIES, SO NO DEVIATION OR DELETION AND EMBELISHMENT OR EXAGGERATION.

The story must be CORRECT AND FACTUAL. So you have to write these stories based on facts that have been gathered by you and/or in some cases by someone else but checked by YOU at least TWICE for correctness. Checking twice can also mean checking it from two different sources. I always give this example.

Say there were some riots outside my friend's shop in a market. He told me 10 people were killed. I will NOT TRUST my friend until someone else also tells me that 10 people were killed or I myself witness 10 dead bodies lying on the street or being hauled by ambulances.

Now when we write news, shall we say "Riots

in New Delhi on Monday left ten people dead" or that "Ten people were killed in the riots in New Delhi on Monday" I prefer the first choice, why, we will discuss in a later chapter.

EASY FOR THE READER TO READ AND CUSTOMERS TO UNDERSTAND

Also the story should be told in way that is easy for the customer to understand. It is the duty of a news writer to keep it simple and easy, especially for radio and TV because if the story is printed in a newspaper, the customers can read it AGAIN, but when told on radio or TV, either they will get it or will not, because there is no reading again in case of radio or TV. So there should be no clauses or complex sentences when we write for the electronic media. If a sentence is becoming too long, break it into two. It will be easy for the news reader to read without losing breath, and also easy for the customer to understand.

EXAMPLE

"Hundreds of protesters, who were demanding higher pay and other benefits, took to the streets in New Delhi on Monday, even after three days of talks with government officials that failed and when police fired tear gas shells to disperse them, they clashed with police and 10 people were killed."

Now this complex sentence is packed with information but too much to read in one sentence. So let us break it up into two sentences.

"Clashes between police and protesters in New Delhi on Monday killed 10 people, as police fired tear gas shells to disperse them. Protesters took to the streets to demand higher pay and other benefits after three days of talks with the government failed."

Here I will insist that a news writer must 'lip

read' the story to check if it is easy to read without any tongue-twisters that would make the presenter fumble as he or she reads it on air.

As I said earlier, news is always about something that happened. Someone did something that has to be told to the world, or said something, or something happened to someone that should not happen to people or the thing that happened was so interesting that other people should know and enjoy a hearty laugh.

You must have heard the expression that when a dog bites a man, it is not news but if a man bites a dog, it is news. So in very simple terms we can say the 'usual' is not news, 'unusual' is news. So if it rained in New Delhi on Monday, it is no news. But if it rained after a long wait, or if it rained so heavily that street drains were clogged and the traffic was affected, it becomes news, because our customers are affected. Another example is that if a government is running the country as it promised before the elections, it is not news (Though I think it should be news because it can assure people and these days good news is also important, but that is my opinion. During my decades-long career, I made sure that every now and then I had a positive story). But if the government breaks the election promises, the news should be all over. Why? It is because our customers are affected. So the news becomes significant for us if our customers are affected in any way and should be presented in a way that they can understand and appreciate.

BACKGROUND INFORMATION FOR PERSPECTIVE

That brings me to the next point. The story

must have enough ADDITIONAL OR AS IT IS CALLED 'BACKGROUND INFORMATION'. If the story is about a brand new event, there may not be a need for any additional information to provide any perspective. But if the brand new event can have some serious consequences in the future, we must add a sentence to say that analysts say it could be so. But remember, the news writer himself or herself cannot predict any consequences. He will have to quote analysts or observers who say the consequences could be serious.

EXAMPLE

This reminds me of a story in a British broadcast about Prime Minister Rajiv Gandhi reshuffling his cabinet in which he got rid of Arun Nehru, who was becoming too powerful in the Congress party.

It said : "In an effort to get rid of his cousin Arun Nehru, a threat to him within the Congress Party, Prime Minister Rajiv Gandhi has reshuffled his cabinet."

I have two objections. First the writer is editorializing by saying "in an effort to", and secondly the sentence is too complex and can be broken into two.

The way I wrote it: *Prime Minister Rajiv Gandhi today reshuffled his cabinet. Analysts say the move was to get rid of his cousin Arun Nehru who was becoming too powerful in the Congress Party and was being seen as a political threat to Mr. Gandhi.*

So in some cases, there is a need to repeat some old or obvious information to reinforce the significance of the story or to give it a perspective so that the customer can really understand its importance. So if the new event has been triggered by something that happened earlier, or someone's comments are in response to something said earlier, or the riots are a backlash of earlier communal fighting then this old information MUST be included at the end of the story or sprinkled as nuggets throughout the story.

EXAMPLE

This was the news story about the price of onions hitting almost 80 rupees a kilo because of a man-made shortage created by hoarders and ignored for weeks by the Congress party government in New Delhi. It looks like a new event and does not need any background.

But if the writer is smart, he or she will remember that the 1980 elections, that brought badly defeated Indira Gandhi back to power, was all about the high prices of onions and potatoes ignored by the then Janata Party government. So this old information gives the required depth and urgency to the story of high onion prices, now being ignored by Congress itself.

COMPLETE, ALL QUESTIONS ANSWERED, ALSO KNOWN AS "BLANKET COVERAGE"

The story must also be COMPLETE, nothing left to the imagination of the customer. It should be told as if the customer knows nothing about it and has never heard about it and is hearing it for the first time. So it should cover EVERY, I mean EVERY angle. There should be no questions left unanswered in the customer's mind about the story. If he or she still has a question, after we present our story, it means we have failed somewhere. I can give tens of examples of wire stories that leave so many questions in my mind. So if you are missing some information and have to file the story on deadline, please say so in simple and honest words *"that the information could not be obtained by the time the story had to be filed or published, but we would try to bring it later."*

EXAMPLE

Recently a lunatic fired at an American politician at a rally somewhere and seriously injured her. The bullet hit her head. TV reports after that simply kept on reporting miraculous progress in her condition at the hospital despite her brain injury. TV reports kept on saying that she was already responding to her doctor's directions, that she also smiled a little when her husband touched her cheek, and that she moved her eyes from right to left etc. But none of the stories said it is still to be seen if she would be able to talk anytime soon. I also had this nagging question in my mind about how serious is the brain injury, until a British TV report ended with this sentence: "But she still cannot talk or walk." Just seven words, but they made the story COMPLETE.

GOOD EXAMPLE

This one is a good example about a story about a notorious multi-storey building scandal in Mumbai. There were many new indictments that followed the original story and every time a story was written about some new people being indicted, it should have had a paragraph about what the scandal was all about. Remember, every time the story has to be told with the assumption that customers are listening to it for the first time. In this example, the reporter weaved the background very carefully in the last graph.

The three main accused in the controversial ABC Housing Society scam were grilled by the CBI for the second day today, seven days after it registered a case against former Maharashtra Chief Minister and 12 others. The three men were confronted with documents seized during searches in January. CBI has indicated that arrest of one of the prime accused in the controversial ABC scam may take place in a couple of days.

According to the First Information Report, two founding members of the ABC society allegedly conspired with others to illegally get the land allotted in favor of the Cooperative Housing Society. The 30-storey building with 105 flats was originally meant for Kargil heroes and their families.

BAD EXAMPLE

Here is a bad example. The Prime Minister is going to address the Commonwealth Law Conference but we don't know what it is about. The reporter just took the government handout and ran it on the wire.

Prime Minister Manmohan Singh will arrive on a two-day visit to the Andhra Pradesh capital tomorrow evening to inaugurate the Commonwealth Law conference to be held at Hyderabad International Convention Centre (HICC) at Madhavpur on Sunday. Singh will reach Begumpet airport from New Delhi at 1945 hrs tomorrow and head to Raj Bhavan.

On February 9, the Prime Minister would proceed to HICC for inaugurating the conference by a helicopter from Begumpet airport at 0900 hrs and reach there at 0920 hrs.

He will leave for New Delhi at 1110 hrs, an official statement said here today.

BALANCED, INCLUDING BOTH SIDES TO THE STORY

The story must also be BALANCED. Remember there are always more than one side to a story. If it is a story on violence, the two sides could be the protesters and the police. If it is a political story, the government and the opposition; If it is a corruption scandal, then the accuser and the accused etc. You will know right away about the two sides and you MUST include both versions. If, for example, you have the account from only one of the two, then say the other side has not responded so far or that you could not obtain the other version. And, of course, if there are more than two sides, then all three sides must be covered.

CHAPTER-2

SIX COMPONENTS OF A NEWS STORY

When you write a story, you can remember it as a "pyramid" divided into six sections. Usually, the top section is the smallest and the sections can get bigger as you move downwards.

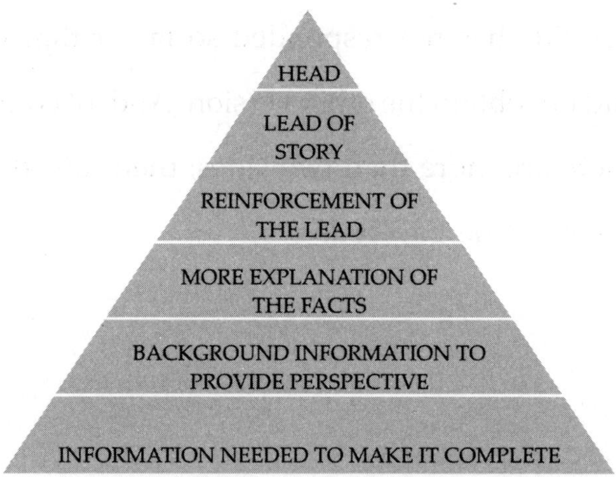

As we talk about the six elements shown in the above "pyramid", remember that sometimes it becomes necessary to change the sequence, but only among the last four elements. For example, sometimes we may have to bring up the "background information" right after the section called "Reinforcement of the lead" to give the lead "more depth and perspective". So remember the sequence of these six elements might be different in some stories, but in order to be "complete", every news story must have these six elements. Just as an exercise, you can take any news story and try to divide it into these six elements. They may be in the above sequence or a little bit different. But you will see that barring the last section, which is included only by the real professionals, all other five elements will be present in every story.

HEADLINE

It is the headline that attracts the attention of the customer. It could be in the newspaper or on radio or on TV or the WEB.

So it should be bold in print or WEB and catchy for radio or TV.

If it is hard news, then there is no problem. ***"Rajiv Gandhi Assassinated by Suspected Tamil Rebels".*** Now this kind of headline will attract anyone's attention because it is hard hitting news that affects everyone and catches their attention right away. But if the story is not hard hitting news, then we will have to make it a teaser, meaning we will have to tease the customer so that he or she feels the story will be interesting but does not have a clue about what it is all about.

GOOD EXAMPLE

There is a story about a trash collector who had found a unique way to sell ordinary trash found on American streets. Once he found a restaurant bill for 500 dollars thrown away by some very rich businessman and a grocery receipt for 3 dollars discarded by a poor person who just bought milk and bread. The innovator compressed the two receipts into one ball in such a way that you could see the two receipts. The balls were of the exact size of a round candy and he sold them through a candy slot machine – one ball for one quarter. So the headline in this case has to be a teaser.

"This is no candy, it is a 'trash for cash' machine"

People will know right away it is about selling trash, but won't be able to imagine the connection between trash and candy and might be lured to see or read the story.

Sometimes, you may have to have a teaser even for hard hitting news.

EXAMPLE

For example, *the news may be about the passage of the government budget by the parliament.* Now the very fact that the budget was passed may not be that interesting to the customer. So the headline can't be just "Parliament Passes the 2010 Budget". It has to be more than that. It should be about something that has a direct impact on the customer's pocket book, and that will attract his or her attention right away. So here it should be a teaser like ***"Sugar, Petrol and Kerosene to Cost More"***. Now the customers will have to pay attention to find out how much more they will have to spend with the new budget.

But a teaser does not mean the headline should be vague and should not give a clue about what the story is all about. We do not need a headline like the one given below from an Indian news agency. You don't know what "solution" they are talking about. Now they may say the minister's name is there, but it just says Ramesh and he can be any one. It is a total waste of a headline.

India to continue work on solution acceptable to all: Ramesh

Environment Minister Jairam Ramesh says despite the ''disappointing'' outcome of the Cancun meet, India would continue to make efforts for a solution to the deadlock in the climate change negotiations. Ramesh also said that not much should be expected from the UN climate conference in Durban too. The Durban meet was scheduled later this year.

Now the lead can be longer than the "headline" because it has to have five W's I was talking about earlier. They are Who, What, Where, Why and When.

To elaborate a little, **W**ho did it, **W**hat happened, **W**here did it happen, **W**hy he did it and **W**hen?

Now all these are questions. And they are the most important questions to begin a story. As I told you all we are going to do is tell the story by answering these questions and some more questions later.

Since we have decided to make the sentences simple and without clauses, we may not be able to pack all five W's in one line. So we can use two sentences. BUT REMEMBER ALL OF THE THREE W'S HAVE TO BE IN THE FIRST SENTENCE OR THE FIRST TWO SENTENCES, NEVER IN THIRD OR FOURTH OR FIFTH. AND NEVER BURY THE LEAD IN THE BOTTOM.

GOOD EXAMPLE

Notice how in this story, all W's are upfront and each graph is just a little over two lines, easy to read and easy to understand:

The United States has called for an "orderly transition" to the new government in Egypt but it stopped short of demanding that President Hosni Mubarak step down as protests engulf his country.

Secretary of State Hillary Clinton hammered home the US position with appearances on news shows and President Barack Obama had used the same language in telephone calls to regional leaders, the White House said.

Mubarak has appointed his military intelligence chief as his first ever vice president and named a new premier to try to assuage his people's thirst for political change, but Clinton said he must go further.

"That is the beginning, the bare beginning of what needs to happen, which is a process that leads to the kind of concrete steps to achieve democratic and economic reforms that we've been urging," she told ABC News.

As the anti-government revolt raged into the seventh day with opposition leader Mohamed ElBaradei addressing protesters in Cairo, Clinton said the Egyptian people should be allowed to pursue "real democracy" through "national dialogue."

The Obama administration has performed a delicate balancing act over the past week, backing reforms but at the same time refusing to cut off vital support for Mubarak's regime.

BAD EXAMPLE

See how long the sentences are. Try to read them in one breath?

Foreign governments have stepped up their warnings on Sunday about travel to Egypt, with several urging their citizens to evacuate as soon as possible amid uncertainty over where the Arab nation is headed.

Egypt's most prominent democracy advocate has called for President Husni Mubarak to resign, speaking to thousands of protesters who defied the curfew for the third night. Fighter jets streaked low overhead and police returned to the capital's streets – high-profile displays of authority over a situation spiraling out of control.

The fears of foreign tourists mirrored those of many Egyptians. Dozens with the means to do so rented jets or hopped aboard their own planes in a mad dash that did little to boost confidence in the future of a country long viewed as a pillar of stability in a restive region. Those leaving included businessmen and celebrities.

ANOTHER GOOD EXAMPLE

For this example, let us use the same news that we wrote earlier about violence in New Delhi.

Clashes between police and protesters in New Delhi on Monday killed 10 people, as police fired tear gas shells to disperse them. Protesters took to the streets to demand higher pay and other benefits after three days of talks with the government failed.

In this case, WHO, WHAT, WHERE AND WHEN are included in the first sentence and WHY in the second. This is fine and acceptable. But remember, either the very FIRST sentence or the FIRST TWO sentences of your story MUST have all the five W's.

Sometimes the lead may be totally different and may not answer any of the five W's. It mainly happens in feature stories, not in the hard news. Just like the catchy headline, this is a catchy lead that highlights an element of a story that the customers can relate to. In the following example, getting the driver's license had to be the headline to catch the reader, and details can come later on in the lead.

EXAMPLE

Getting the driving license issued or renewed just got easier

The Delhi Government has put in place a system that allows you to apply for your driving license from any of its 15 zonal offices.

A smart card based driving license issue system of Delhi Integrated Multi-Modal Transit System was today inaugurated by Delhi's Chief Minister.

DITS has centralized all the driving license data

facilitating the applicants to get the new licenses issued or renew their old ones from any of the 15 zonal offices, an official release said.

The new system also allows applicants to fix an appointment in advance to visit the office and avoid waiting in the queue.

Under the new system, the applicant's identity will be re-verified through fingerprint matching before he/she is allowed to sit for the learner license test.

REINFORCEMENT OF THE LEAD

This portion of the story has all those details that should have been included in the first two sentences but were left out because of the limited space and the necessity of specifying the five W's.

This part reinforces the lead, meaning gives more information to pad up the lead.

Just in the above example – the drivers' license story – you will notice the first paragraph is the lead that follows the headline and the sentence after that reinforces the lead, saying how and why it can be reissued anywhere.

EXAMPLE

To continue the example of the "New Delhi Violence" story, this portion can quote a police official or a hospital official or a protester as saying that at least 10 people were killed and so many were injured and how serious the injuries are. And do we expect the death toll to go up etc.

MORE EXPLANATION OF THE FACTS

Here we can give more details of how the people gathered and how the demonstration was peaceful at first. Then came hundreds of more people and one of them was roughed up by the police. Then police fired tear gas shells to disperse the crowd after some of them started throwing rocks at the riot police. And then you can say how the clashes began that left 10 people dead. You will have to be careful in saying who clashed first, the protesters or the police. This part can also have a quote from or the sound bite of a police officer explaining the reason of the clashes and to balance the story, a bite of a protester explaining how the clashes began.

BACKGROUND INFORMATION

This is a tricky part. The background information should be enough to inform the customer of some earlier or historical facts, but not too much to make the customer feel that he or she is stupid.

GOOD EXAMPLE

As you know not many Westerners know much about Myanmar or Burma and its famous opposition leader Aung San Suu Kyi. But this story gives all the relevant background information to make even a young student understand what is happening in Burma:

Burma's military government is set to convene its first session of parliament in more than two decades on Monday.

The formation of a national parliament in the capital of Naypyitaw in central Burma, far from major population centers, takes the country toward the final stage of the government's self-proclaimed transition to democracy. But the legislature will be composed almost entirely of military allies. One quarter of the parliamentary seats already were reserved for military nominees even before the November national elections. And the government-backed Union Solidarity and Development Party won nearly 80 percent of the remaining seats.

Critics say a parliament without the opposition National League for Democracy party (NLD) headed by Nobel laureate Aung San Suu Kyi cannot lay legitimate claim to democratic labels or ideals.

The NLD won a landslide elections victory in 1990, but the military refused to recognize those results. In other developments, the NLD launched a website on Sunday aimed at broadening its reach.

Aung San Suu Kyi described the website as a chance for her party to reach a goal of "democratic union at a faster pace."

The move came just two days after a special court rejected her appeal to reinstate her political party, which was forced to dissolve last year after it boycotted parliamentary elections. In announcing the boycott, the NLD said it was protesting a decree from the military government banning convicted felons from joining political parties. Critics say the ban was aimed at keeping Aung San Suu Kyi, who spent years under house arrest for her pro-democracy activities, from gaining political office.

To continue the New Delhi violence story as an example, we can compare the pay-scales of the government employees with similar workers in a private outfit. Or if this is the second time these employees are protesting for higher wages we can tell our customers what happened after the first demonstration. Were there any talks between the government and the unions? Did they succeed or failed? What was promised and how much was delivered by the government the first time, what were the new events that led to the second demonstration, etc.

ANOTHER GOOD EXAMPLE

Here is a story in which, until the last paragraph about the militants was added, the story was incomplete because you don't know the reason and the motive of the attack.

Five police officers were killed and one injured in an attack by unidentified gunmen in Russia's volatile North Caucasus republic of Kabardino-Balkaria. The gunmen yesterday broke into a cafe in the town of Chegem where road traffic police officers were having lunch and shot them execution style, a spokesman for the federal investigative committee told the news agency. Four policemen died on the spot and the fifth was hospitalized. A criminal investigation has been opened.

Attacks by militants on police and security officials are frequent in Russia's Muslim-dominated volatile North Caucasus Republics as the federal authorities have been clamping down on militant groups.

INFORMATION THAT IS NOT AVAILABLE TO ANSWER ALL QUESTIONS

This section of the story is self-explanatory and sometimes you may have all the information, so it may not be needed. But the news writer should really spend some time in considering if this section is needed or not. Read your story and see if all the questions have been answered. You become the customer and ask yourself if you want to know anything more about the story. If you are sure the story is complete, you are done. If you think here are some questions that have not been answered, make more phone calls and if you cannot obtain an answer to a particular doubt in your mind, just say so.

GOOD EXAMPLE

Notice below in the last paragraph how the reporter tells us what was not clear at the time he or she wrote the story, and also that more floods and deaths can be expected.

Bolivian authorities reported on Sunday that at least 29 people died when flood waters swept away a passenger bus and a truck in southeastern Bolivia.

The incident happened late Friday near the town of Pampahuasi, on the banks of the Mollepunku River, about 600 kilometers southeast of Bolivia's capital La Paz.Several people are still missing.

The police chief of Chuquisaca region said 49 people were in the bus. Two people were in the truck's cabin, and it is unclear if the vehicles had any other passengers. The numbers suggest that the death toll could rise in the coming days as bodies wash up on the river banks. More floods are expected as forecasters predict more rain.

SOME OTHER PRACTICAL HINTS

SPELL IT OUT

While writing for Radio or TV, always spell out the amount because it is not easy for the newsreader to calculate the amount as he or she reads the news.

EXAMPLE

Don't write Rupees 6,00,000. Instead, say six-lakh or six-hundred-thousand Rupees. The hyphens are my personal preference. If I want the newsreader to read three or four words together as one word, I always hyphenate them. This is not good for Print journalism, but for Broadcast we can and should take liberty to make it easy for the newsreader to read our story.

DON'T USE ABBREVIATIONS

You will find news in India full of abbreviations and the writers take the easy way out and just use the abbreviations, leaving customers like me to wonder what he or she is talking about. Even a Joint Parliamentary Committee is abbreviated to JPC.

The rule is that you must use the full name in the lead, along with the abbreviation in parenthesis, and then use the abbreviation JPC in the sentences that follow the lead. Now this rule may be good for print media only because in a TV or Radio story, if you missed the lead where it was explained what JPC is, you will never know even after the news ends, what JPC is.

ALWAYS CHECK PRONUNCIATION OF NAMES

Remember if you interview someone for your TV or Radio story where the presenter has to pronounce the name of a person, please ask him or her for the pronunciation at the time of the interview. It may create a problem later for the newsreader if you don't do your footwork. And needless to say it is the sacred duty of the anchor to check the pronunciations before he or she goes in front of the camera. Today on Indian channels if you pay attention you will see that sometimes the same name is pronounced differently by the anchor and a minute later differently by the reporter in the field.

CHAPTER-3

WHY WRITING FOR TV IS A SPECIALITY

Now that we have figured out how to construct a basic news story, let us discuss what the TV News story looks like today.

TV news these days mostly consists of TV packages produced by the reporter/producer that contain footage about the news event and a couple of sound-bites of the people linked to the event. So to make it easy to understand, in the layman's words, the package can be divided into two sections. One is where you as a reporter have to read your report and the other is where you are quiet and to report the story you are using the selected sound-bites of the people you interviewed.

So when you use the sound-bite the face of the person interviewed is on the screen. But when you are telling the story, for that part **your face** will be on the screen. So in order to avoid a situation where you are seen again and again in the story, you can show the footage of the event with your voice in the background. You can track your voice before you edit the story and cover most of your voice with the footage of that story. This footage can be the one you shot to cover the story or can be from the Tape library. Whatever it is, it is called the B-roll. And the main footage of the interviews for the story is called the A-roll.

So the sound-bites etc. are the A-roll that will be seen as such, and the set up shots of the interviewees and different shots about the event or about your analytical story are the B-roll that would cover your narration.

And in the end you show yourself standing at the scene saying a few sentences before you sign off. That, in TV terminology is called "Piece to Camera"

EXAMPLE

Say it is a story about the fire in an office building. You will open the story with the best footage of the fire, then show a different footage of the fire etc. when you talk about the fire and its probable causes. Then you talk to a witness or two who will tell you what they saw and then you show a firefighter saying how difficult it was to enter the building and put it out. And in the end you show yourself standing in front of the building, saying the last few sentences.

Now depending on the story, some stories have all the footage and no sound-bites or some can be mostly sound-bites with very little footage.

EXAMPLE

Say the story is about the illegal construction of a high-rise building in Mumbai. In this, you can only show the building, the department or the ministry that gives permits for construction, suspects who built the building and the owners who now have the risk of losing a lot of money. If someone is ready to talk in front of the camera, you would have a better story but if not, then you will show everything without a sound-bite.

Another possibility is that you get all the sound-bites – those of the ministry officials, of the builder and also of the owners. In that case this will become a story dominated by sound-bites with very little footage.

So the quality of the story depends on whether you could get the relevant interviews in time, whether your cameraman got good B-roll of the news event and how well you presented it.

Now let us discuss the real differences between writing news for the print media and writing it for the electronic media or say for broadcast on Radio and TV, or for Web-casts.

Some say a news story is a news story, so how could it be written in one way for newspapers and in another for Radio and TV.

You won't believe I had to face this question when, as a member of the Board of Advisers on Curriculum of a respected University famous for its courses on Journalism, I asked them to split the News-writing course into two – Basic News-writing and News-writing for Radio and TV. They had only one category, simply that of "News writing". I proposed it should be two separate categories – one for print and another for TV and

Radio. One of the members challenged me to show them why they need two separate courses because that would involve two separate teachers. I said they probably will not need two separate teachers if they hire an experienced teacher to begin with.

I said the magic lies in the choice of the most appropriate words and the way the sentences are constructed. For print we can write a basic story we learnt in earlier chapters. But for Radio we have to paint a visual picture of the situation, whereas for TV and WEB, we already have the visuals, so we have to very smartly avoid saying the same thing that we are showing on the screen. So I gave the following example of how the news will be written for different mediums about the recent uprising in Egypt:

LEAD FOR PRINT

Thousands of Egyptians demonstrated in Cairo Monday demanding that President Husni Mubarak end his 30 year regime and leave the country. They complained that so far Mubarak's inept and corrupt regime has not done anything for the people – from creating jobs or basic development of the country to bring prosperity to the people.

FOR RADIO

Now for Radio you have to paint a picture for the listener by describing the action. You must have listened to the Radio Plays that used to be broadcast by All India Radio or other channels. In those plays when the characters say their dialogues, everything else is left to your imagination. But that imagination is dictated by the words uttered by the actors who try to convey the feelings through their voices. In the news, everything depends on the "words" and "sentences" because the newscasters are not supposed to act it out but read it a neutral way with a detached authority in their voices.

"Thousands of Egyptians took to the streets in Cairo Monday....etc". Here we use the words "took to the streets" to show action and movement, instead of just using the word "demonstrated".

FOR TELEVISION

Now in TV there is no need to "paint a picture" because we are showing the picture already on the screen. In this case the customer is watching on the screen that thousands of Egyptians are on the streets protesting the regime. So, here as they watch the demonstrations, the clashes and the running battles, we can talk about their demands, how the demonstrations began or the response of the government to the charges of corruption etc. As you know it is very difficult to have a decent footage about the government corruption other than showing the officials who have been allegedly corrupt. So we can use the dramatic footage of the demonstrations to say what they are protesting against. This requires a lot of planning on the producer's part.

NOW NOTICE HOW DIFFERENT THE WRITING IS FOR TV

As we show the protests on the screen, the anchor says:

"These people in Cairo are demanding jobs, prosperity from Husni Mubarak's regime which they say has been inept and corrupt for 30 years, not doing

anything for the people. They started gathering in downtown Cairo in the early hours of Monday, perhaps inspired by the similar demonstrations held in neighboring Tunisia."

This example brings me to a very significant difference in news writing for PRINT and for TV that is based on some of the basic principles we discussed earlier, such as the principle of five "W's" in the lead. In print and Radio, we have to describe in vivid and visual terms "what" happened before we say "why" it happened. Whereas in TV we can describe the "why" at the same time we show on the screen "what" happened and "where it happened".

CHAPTER-4

SOME SPECIAL TOUCHES FOR TV STORIES

So now that you have got the idea as to what really is the basic difference between writing for the Print or Radio and writing for TV , we can talk about the special touches we can give in writing a TV story to catch the rapt attention of our customers by making it better written and also visually better .

YOU WANT TO OPEN THE STORY WITH THE BEST VIDEO CLIP YOU HAVE

Now it may happen that somehow you missed the best shot. If you did and you want to use file footage to make it more dramatic, make sure you introduce your piece as a backgrounder.

So write the main lead to be read by the anchor, and begin your story with a little history and then come back to the main story. But there are precautions to take if you do that.

BE 100 % HONEST ABOUT THE FOOTAGE

Say the story is about terrorism and you are opening your story with the blast that happened two days ago. So say, "there have been a number of attacks in recent days, just two days ago this blast took place," and then come to the latest story. Don't pretend the blast you are showing on the screen is today's by not specifying the timing and letting the customers presume that it must have happened today. Also when we use any old footage, the screen must prominently show the words "FILE", either on the left hand or the right hand corner. And please DO NOT add background music to the old footage.

NO PLACE FOR MUSIC IN A NEWS STORY, ONLY NATS

Please DO NOT use background music, as many TV channels have been doing, to separate the old footage from the new. There is no place for background music in a News story. If you add music, it becomes a news feature, a documentary or sorry to say just "fiction". The moment you add music, you are telling the customers that what they are watching is not the actual news but a dramatized version produced by us in the studios.

PLEASE SHOOT WITH THE LEAD IN MIND

As we have discussed, you need the best shot

to open your story and that should be on your mind when you are covering a story. You can shoot different angles of the story and may have all the footage you need. But while your cameraman is shooting the story, your mind should be working on the lead and you should find out on the scene if your shooter has that scene that you are going to use for the lead. If not, tell the shooter to shoot it again from that angle. This may be more relevant especially when your story is not hard news but a feature. You cannot shoot a good non-newsy feature story until you know exactly how you are going to begin the story. You may have that in your mind already or it might come to you while shooting the piece from different angles.

AND ALSO YOU SHOULD BE THINKING ABOUT HOW YOU PLAN TO EDIT THE VIDEO AS YOU SHOOT

Film directors always say, when you shoot a scene, editing should always be on your mind. What they mean is that if you know how you are going to edit the scene, you will not miss the shot you are going to need when you are editing the story. I think this is also most relevant while shooting a news story. The cameraman will never know how you are going to write the story and what B-roll you will need for that. Remember the sound-bites are fine, but to cover your narration you will require the appropriate B-roll and if you don't have that, then you will have to compromise on your story by skipping that part.

EXAMPLE

Say you are covering a story about fire at a gas

station or a petrol pump that engulfed a huge area in downtown New Delhi. No one knows how the fire began but you notice a welding shop very close to the pump. You might say in your story that sparks from that shop could trigger a fire. Unless you have the shot showing the proximity of the welding sparks to the pump, you won't be able to add that significant angle to your story.

WRITE YOUR SCRIPT ACCORDING TO THE VIDEO CLIPS THAT GO WITH IT

This is more relevant when you have to write a news story for which you were not on the scene with a cameraman. That means someone else covered the story but somehow it fell into your lap and you will now have to write around the footage you got, good or bad. For this you must view the whole footage very carefully and take notes and then decide how you are going to write the story. Hopefully, you will have all the B-roll you need. If not, you must craft the story in a way that no one notices the lack of it.

This also becomes true when you are using some Tape library footage to provide background in order to give depth to your story.

EXAMPLE

Say you are writing a story about a Naxalite attack in the state of Orissa. After showing that attack, you want to say similar attacks were also reported last week in two neighboring states. When you use the old footage, you will have to write "to the video" that is already there.

DON'T SAY EXACTLY WHAT YOU ARE SHOWING ON THE SCREEN

This precaution cannot be overemphasized. We don't do that for many reasons, but two are the most prominent. One is to save time and the second is not to seem repetitive and pedantic. As we know most of the TV stories in a News bulletin cannot be more than a minute long or maximum minute-and-a-half. So to save time, we can use what is being seen on the screen to discuss other elements of the story.

EXAMPLE

To use the most familiar example, in a story about protest demonstrations, we do not have to repeat that hundreds of people took to the streets in downtown Mumbai to demonstrate. Instead when the picture of the demonstrators comes on the screen, we can say *"these people were demonstrating against the sudden hike in the price of onions due to a man-made shortage."* We can use that time-slot for saying the demonstrators are blaming the price rise on the hoarders etc.

Another reason for that is not to sound boring and repetitive.

EXAMPLE

I remember one of my stories on Benazir Bhutto's political comeback in Pakistan, in which I spoke about her house-arrest in Pakistan. The video showed her house cordoned off by barbed wire and surrounded by police. In my narration I said that she is under house arrest because she has become the most serious political threat for the military leader in power. My Western copy-editor, who was not familiar with her house etc., insisted that I should write that this is Bhutto's house that has been cordoned off by police and the security around it has been tightened. I put my foot down and refused to change my script. I just told him "we don't have to repeat in words what the picture is already showing" and he had to agree with me and leave the script as it was.

USE SHORT SENTENCES AND TRY TO CHANGE THE B-ROLL AT THE END OF EVERY SENTENCE, JUST LIKE A BEAT IN MUSIC

The most important secret of writing a script for a TV story lies in the length of the sentences as you unfold the story. If you want to make a story pithy and hard hitting, try to write really short sentences when you open the story, and change the shot at the beat of one-two-three, meaning changing the shot on every third beat. As you know, the attention span these days is very short.

EXAMPLE

Say the story is about a terrorist attack on the Red Fort in New Delhi. You can simply write a long sentence saying:

"Unknown gunmen opened fire at a gift shop inside the Red Fort in New Delhi Tuesday, despite tight security at the main gate."

Or you can make three separate sentences, changing shots each time with a new sentence.

The Historic Red Fort in New Delhi, (show the fort on the screen)

Unknown gunmen somehow hoodwinked the tight security at the main gate Tuesday, (show the main gate and security)

And minutes later, opened fire at this gift shop

inside the fort, (show the gift shop).

I hope you get the drift. What I did was very simple. I built a montage of shots with brief sentences to make it more dramatic.

DO NOT INTRODUCE A SOUND BITE BY REPEATING EXACTLY WHAT THE PERSON SAYS IN THE BITE

This is the most common trap the TV news writers fall into these days. If you watch news on different channels, and pay close attention to what I am going to tell you, you will be amazed at how many channels are doing it every day.

Obviously, if it is a breaking story, it is understandable if there is repetition. That can happen on any channel. But if it is a story normally produced for a news bulletin with enough time at hand, **there is no excuse for the anchor to repeat the reporter's lead "word by word".**

EXAMPLE

News anchor: *Prime Minister Manmohan Singh's visit to Paris has been postponed by one week. Now he will fly to Paris on the 19th of this month. So and so has a report.*

Reporter: *Prime Minister Manmohan Singh's visit to Paris has been postponed by one week. Now he will go to Paris on the 19th of this month.*

Now whosoever wrote the anchor's line just repeated what the reporter was going to say any way.

A better way is given below, and notice how easy it is to make it better.

News anchor: *Prime Minister Manmohan Singh*

changes the dates of his visit to Paris. So and so has the details.

Reporter: *Prime Minister Manmohan Singh's visit to Paris has been postponed by one week. Now he will go to Paris on the 19th of this month.*

END WITH SUCH A POWERFUL VIDEO THAT IT LINGERS IN THE MEMORY OF THE WATCHER

As ideally we want to begin our TV package with the best shot we have, we also want to end the piece with a shot that can linger for long in the memory of our customers. This is not always possible but we should strive for this. Also if the shot is really good, plan on omitting a stand up in the end. You can do a "bridge" in the middle of the story where you are seen on the screen just as you stand but the bridge is not at the end but somewhere in the middle to advance the story. This comes in really handy when you don't have the proper B-roll for a few sentences. So instead of the B-roll, you can show yourself saying something for which you can't show pictures or you can be seen in the sound bite of someone you interviewed, sitting with him or her or walking along as he or she says something.

So there are two common examples where you don't want to do a stand up in the end. One, when the last shot can be memorable. And two, when you have to say something in the middle of the story but you don't have the proper B-roll to cover it. So in that case you can use the "bridge technique" and be seen in the middle of the story.

EXAMPLE

This is an example of how you can ruin the last

shot by doing a stand up. *One of my reporters was doing a story about F-18 fighter jets and got excellent DVD from the relevant company's Publicity office. They had spent huge sums of money to produce that DVD, with one of the shots in which the F-18 was flying during Sunset and the dramatic footage was shot from another plane flying close to the F-18. It was a fascinating shot of the plane flying in the twilight. My reporter used that shot at the Sunset as his last shot, but then came himself on camera to do his stand up or as they say "piece to camera". It was so abrupt and seemed so awkward when suddenly from the F-18 in the twilight, we hit the ground where our reporter was doing his stand up in the bright daylight. What a jolt !!*

CHAPTER-5

EXAMPLES FOR STUDENTS

[WARNING: THE FACTS AND NAMES IN THESE SAMPLES AND NEWS WRITING EXERCISES ARE NOT REAL]

Now that we have discussed specific tools and techniques to write News stories without falling into the usual traps, it is high time to identify them in actual examples to hone our skill. I have tried to bring you varied examples for exercising your skills, but you can also do this by reading any newspaper stories or watching them on TV, and then breaking them up into different sections according to our pyramid and then finding out if you feel the story is COMPLETE or whether certain questions still remained unanswered in your mind. Also try to see if you could have written the story in a different way or if you could have improved the story according to what you have learnt so far. You will be amazed when you find out that many of the stories will fall short of the principles we discussed so far.

Pasted below is the screen shot of a real-time news item where each part is tagged for clear understanding *(go to last page for clearer image):*

Disclosure scheme for foreign assets soon

WIN-WIN To cover NRIs too; lower taxes, legal immunity on offer

Debobrat Ghose

NEW DELHI: The government is working out the details of a voluntary income disclosure scheme that would offer a window for bringing back undisclosed assets stashed away in overseas tax havens into the country's financial system.

The Offshore Voluntary Compliance Scheme will cover Indian organisations, citizens and non-resident Indians (NRIs), and offer immunity from criminal prosecution and imprisonment, besides lower rates of interest and penalties.

Also, the authorities will not insist on disclosure of the source of money once it is done voluntarily. But in case the tax department tracks down undisclosed assets through its networks, the holder of the money would face "strong punitive actions, including high penalties, prosecution and even imprisonment", said a government source.

The last such offer — the Voluntary Disclosure of Income Scheme (VDIS), introduced in 1997 to fight internal black money generation — was an unconventional, but successful one. More than 350,000 people disclosed their income and assets under the scheme that brought in ₹7,800 crore. The scheme was closed on December 31, 1998.

An expert group of the Central Board of Direct Taxes (CBDT), assigned by the government to curb the generation and transfer of black money abroad and bring the funds back, recommended the new scheme.

The source said, "It ... modeled on the ... Offshore Volu... Initiative run ... Revenue Servi... ...us."

Under attack by civil society and social activist Anna Hazare for alleged inaction over money stashed away in foreign accounts, the government ... posed an action pla... amendment ... other ... ...com- ...ink-tanks ...ional Institute ... Finance and Policy, ...ional Institute of Financial Management and the National Council for Applied Economic Research — has been set up to estimat... the quantum of black mo... ...ated in India.

...erim recommen... ...P task force esti... ... amount generated ... independence at $500 billion (about ₹22.5 lakh crore) to $1.4 trillion (about ₹63 lakh crore).

A recent study by Global Financial Integrity, a Washington-based research group, estimated the current value of illicit money outflow from India at $462 billion (about ₹20.79 lakh crore).

A FRESH BAIT

- The Offshore Voluntary Compliance Scheme will offer Indian organisations and citizens, including NRIs, the chance to pay taxes on slush funds parked in foreign bank accounts
- It will be modeled on the lines of Offshore Voluntary Disclosure Initiative run by the US Internal Revenue Service
- The last such offer — Voluntary Disclosure of Income Scheme — was launched in 1997
- An expert group of the Central Board of Direct Taxes recommended the scheme
- Govt commissioned a study by think-tanks NIPFP, NIFM and NCAER to estimate the size of India's black economy

INDIA'S BLACK MONEY ESTIMATE

A BJP task force estimated the amount at $500 billion (about **₹22.5 lakh crore**) to $1.4 trillion (about **₹63 lakh crore**)

Global Financial Integrity, a Washington-based research group, estimated the present value of illicit money outflow from India at $462 billion (**₹20.79 lakh crore**)

So here are some more examples for you to sharpen your skills.

The first Indian evacuees from chaos-stricken Libya

have arrived in New Delhi, telling reporters of robberies, looting and narrow escapes from spiraling violence as the revolt intensified.

An Air India flight with 300 evacuees from Libya arrived at the airport in the Indian capital late Saturday.

One of the evacuees Prem Sharma told reporters at the airport, "the situation in Libya is very bad," adding that "all the police stations have been burnt down." He said many Indians had gone without fresh food and water for a week.

Fears of a full-scale civil war in Libya have prompted several countries to scramble to charter ships and planes to get their citizens out.

IN THIS STORY, THE LEAD IS A THREE BARREL LEAD. JUST THE LEAD TELLS YOU THAT THE FIRST INDIAN EVACUEES FROM

LIBYA ARE SAFELY BACK IN INDIA, THAT THERE THEY WERE ROBBED AND ALSO THAT THE REVOLT HAS INTENSIFIED AND VIOLENCE HAS INCREASED. THE LEAD IS SO GOOD AND INFORMATIVE THAT IT DOESN'T MATTER THAT THE WRITER MENTIONS THE NUMBER OF EVACUEES IN THE SECOND PARAGRAPH.

HERE IS AN EXAMPLE OF A BAD LEAD

Western powers have proposed an arms embargo, travel ban and assets freeze on Gaddafi, his family and top ministers and military officials.

But the proposal did not get enough votes for approval because of one controversial clause. The disagreement among members was triggered by their move to refer the Libya crackdown to the International Criminal Court (ICC) for possible crimes against humanity.

Diplomats said China, Russia, South Africa, India, Brazil and Portugal have raised various concerns about ICC involvement.

"There are various levels of concern and this (the ICC) is the main sticking point," said a council diplomat, speaking on condition of anonymity.

French and Britain played a key role in drafting the resolution. But the diplomat said, "On the arms embargo no problem, on the sanctions no problem, the only question which is still on the table is the way we are going to reference to the ICC."

The Security Council's main members (the United States, China, Russia and India) do not belong to the ICC and have always viewed it with suspicion.

The Security Council so far has only referred the Darfur conflict to the ICC and Sudan's President was charged with war crimes and genocide.

NOW IN THIS STORY THE LEAD IS BURIED IN THE SECOND PARAGRAPH. THE SECURITY COUNCIL HAS PROPOSED SEVERAL ACTIONS AGAINST THE LIBYAN RULER BUT THE REAL NEWS IS THAT THE PROPOSAL COULD NOT BE PASSED BECAUSE OF ONE HITCH AND THAT IS ON THE ICC. THE WHOLE STORY IS ABOUT THAT HITCH BUT THE LEAD OF THE STORY IS "WRONG" BECAUSE IT DOES NOT MENTION THE CONTROVERSY AT ALL.

AND HERE IS ANOTHER EXAMPLE OF THE SAME STORY IN WHICH THE LEAD IS BURIED IN THE LAST PARAGRAPH:

UN Security Council envoys on Saturday embarked on tough negotiations over how to sanction

Libyan leader Moammar Qaddafi for his deadly offensive on opposition protesters.

Western nations have proposed sanctions that include an arms embargo and travel ban and assets freeze on Qaddafi, his family and top ministers.

But diplomats said China, Russia, South Africa, India and other nations have expressed various levels of concern about a proposal to refer the Libya crackdown to the International Criminal Court for possible crimes against humanity investigation.

ANOTHER EXAMPLE OF HOW A TV STORY IS WRITTEN DIFFERENTLY

Hundreds of people staged a noisy anti-American protest outside the US Consulate in the eastern Pakistani city of Lahore on Saturday chanting, "Any friend of America is a traitor."

They burned a US flag and set fire to an effigy of an American CIA contractor accused of murdering two Pakistanis in Lahore on January 27.

The US Embassy says Raymond Davis shot the men in self defense because they tried to rob him. He has been in jail since the January incident.

Saturday's demonstration was organized by the Jamaat-ud-Dawa, an alleged front for the banned militant group Lashkar-e-Toiba.

Lashkar-e-Toiba is blamed in the deadly 2008 attacks in Mumbai, India, and Pakistan's government insists it has cracked down on it and its affiliated groups.

NOTE VERY CAREFULLY. IF THIS WAS A TV STORY, THE WAY THE FIRST TWO PARAGRAPHS HAVE BEEN WRITTEN WILL CHANGE. THE REASON: WE WILL BE

SHOWING THEM CHANTING THE SLOGANS SO WE DON'T HAVE TO SPELL THEM OUT AND WE WILL SAY "HERE THEY ARE BURNING THE EFFIGY OF SO AND SO". SO HERE JUST THE STYLE OF WRITING THIS NEWS ITEM WILL CHANGE SLIGHTLY. THE FACTS WILL NOT CHANGE BUT THE WORDINGS WILL CHANGE BECAUSE WE DON'T WANT TO REPEAT IN WORDS, EXACTLY WHAT WE ARE ALREADY SHOWING ON THE SCREEN.

The head of India's state-run National Aluminum Company was arrested on Saturday on bribery charges, heaping fresh embarrassment on the scandal-tainted Congress government.

The NALCO chairman ....

THIS LEAD IS A GOOD DOUBLE BARREL

LEAD. BUT THE WRITER SHOULD HAVE PUT THE ABBREVIATED NAME (NALCO) IN THE LEAD AFTER THE FULL NAME, INDICATING THAT FROM NOW ON WE WILL CALL THE COMPANY "NALCO". FOR THE NEWSPAPER IT IS FINE THE WAY IT IS WRITTEN BECAUSE THE READER CAN GO BACK TO THE LEAD OR THE FIRST PARAGRAPH TO FIND OUT WHAT NALCO STANDS FOR. BUT IF IT IS A RADIO OR TV STORY, WE CANNOT TAKE A SECOND LOOK AT THE FIRST PARAGRAPH TO FIND OUT WHAT THE ABBREVIATION STANDS FOR.

EXAMPLE OF AN INCOMPLETE STORY

Three attacks on civilians in Afghanistan have left at least 10 people dead and 25 others injured.

A suicide bomber detonated a bomb at a sports field

in northern Afghanistan on Saturday, killing one person and wounding 25 others. Taliban fighters are now attacking mainly civilian targets in order to inflict as many casualties as they can and instill fear.

No one claimed responsibility for Saturday's incident.

NOW THIS STORY IS A DISASTER. THE LEAD TALKS ABOUT THREE ATTACKS, THE STORY TELLS ABOUT ONLY ONE SUICIDE BOMBER ATTACK. IT SAYS IN THE LEAD SOME 10 PEOPLE WERE KILLED BUT THE SUICIDE BOMB KILLED ONLY ONE PERSON. SO THE NUMBERS DON'T MATCH. IT SAYS IT HAPPENED IN NORTHERN AFGHANISTAN, BUT THERE IS NO TOWN OR CITY OR VILLAGE MENTIONED. THE NEWS WRITER DOES NOT ATTRIBUTE THE THIRD PARAGRAPH ABOUT THE TALIBAN

CHANGING THEIR APPROACH, SO HE IS EDITORIALIZING BY INSERTING HIS OR HER COMMENT.

THE FOLLOWING STORY IS A TYPICAL EXAMPLE OF HOW THE ANCHOR SAYS THE SAME THING WHICH THE CORRESPONDENT IN THE FIELD IS GOING TO REPEAT. NOTICE THE REPETITION AND TRY TO WRITE WHAT THE INTRODUCTION SHOULD BE BY THE ANCHOR AND HOW THE REPORTER IN THE FIELD SHOULD START HIS OR HER STORY.

Anchor: *Some 80 per cent of northern Afghan Border Police [ABP] forces have been equipped with modern weapons. Mohammad Jalali, commander of northern border zone, said nearly 15,000 new weapons had been brought into the country, saying a quantity of these weapons would also be given to the ABP forces in the north zone of the country. Jalali expressed satisfaction over the security situation in northern zone borders.*

Correspondent: *The border forces have been equipped with new weapons. Mohammad Jalali, commander of northern border zone, while making these comments on the 14th ABP officers' graduation, added they had distributed the new weapons to 80 per cent of the ABP forces in this zone so far and they would resume the process next year as well.*

JALALI BITE

"Almost 80 per cent of our [required] weapons have been swapped with better weapons and we issue them to our checkpoints and they are intending to complete the remaining ones by next year."

SO NOW THE FIGURE "80 PERCENT OF THE WEAPONS" WAS FIRST REPORTED BY

THE ANCHOR, THEN THE REPORTER AND THEN THE BITE ALSO SAYS THE SAME THING. THIS REPETITION IS TOO MUCH.

APPLY THE "PYRAMID" IN THE FOLLOWING STORY:

Police say contaminated intravenous fluid is suspected in the deaths of twelve pregnant women at a government hospital in northwestern India.

Hospital officials say doctors are battling to save the lives of four more women who fell critically ill after being given the fluid in the maternity ward.

Police are investigating the manufacturer and distributors of the contaminated I-V fluid after the young women died over the past 10 days in a government hospital in Jodhpur.

Authorities seized the remaining bottles of fluid in the hospital after laboratory tests confirmed that some of them were tainted with fungus and bacteria. Health officials are also inspecting the hospital's operating rooms and the maternity ward for infections.

Police say the company has been asked to withdraw its I-V fluid stocks from all over the country.

Tens of thousands of women die in India each year during pregnancy or childbirth because of limited access to emergency care.

NOW IN THE STORY THAT FOLLOWS, I HAVE PURPOSELY BURIED THE LEAD. TRY TO FIND THE LEAD AND THEN REWRITE THE STORY

Russian Deputy Foreign Minister Sergei Ryabkov says 16 percent of weapons, military hardware and servicemen sent by the United States to Afghanistan cross Russian territory.

He told the parliament 16 percent of military hardware and weapons forwarded by the U.S. to Afghanistan transit the Russian territory. The information available indicates that a further 9% reach Afghanistan, through Ukraine, Georgia and countries in the Middle East.

On Friday the chamber began debating a bill ratifying a Russian-U.S. agreement permitting the transit of weapons, *military hardware, military property and personnel across Russian territory to support Washington's role in security and stabilization efforts in Afghanistan.*

The document was signed by the Russian and U.S. presidents in Moscow in 2009, and it began applying 90 days after it was signed.

Ryabkov said a total of 95,000 U.S. Servicemen

and more than 29 tons of cargo bound for Afghanistan have already crossed Russian territory as part of the agreement. "The agreement allows us to produce a serious influence on the work of the U.S. and NATO on the aforementioned topic," he said.

He told parliamentarians from the Communist Party that not a single U.S. airplane so far has landed on the Russian territory.

A BETTER WAY TO WRITE THIS STORY WOULD BE AS FOLLOWS:

The Russian Parliament has begun debating a bill ratifying a Russian-U.S. agreement permitting the transit of weapons, military hardware and personnel across the Russian territory.

The agreement is aimed at supporting Washington's role in security and stabilization efforts in Afghanistan.

The accord was signed by the Russian and U.S. presidents in Moscow in 2009.

Russian Deputy Foreign Minister Sergei Ryabkov told the chamber that sixteen percent of weapons, military hardware and servicemen sent by the United States to Afghanistan cross the Russian territory.

He said more than 95-thousand U.S. servicemen and more than 29 tons of cargo bound for Afghanistan have already crossed Russian territory as part of the agreement.

He also noted that the agreement allows us to influence the work of the U.S. and NATO in this regard.

He said not a single US plane so far has landed on Russian territory.

LOOK AT THE CLUTTER IN THE FOLLOWING STORY

The naval forces of as many as 39 countries have confirmed their participation in the Exercise AMAN (Peace)-11 to be conducted in North Arabian Sea from August 8 to 11.

A senior official told newsmen on Thursday, "We have received confirmation from 39 out of the 47 countries invited to the event." This is the third exercise of AMAN series with slogan "Together for Peace".

The first exercise of AMAN series was held in March 2005. During AMAN-05, 14 ships of Bangladesh, China, France, Italy, Malaysia, UK and USA navies participated.

The second Exercise AMAN-07 was held in March 2006. During this exercise, 33 ships, 23 aircraft and 10

SOF teams of Australia, Bangladesh, China, France, Japan, Malaysia, UK and Nigeria, Turkey and USA participated. Observers from 27 countries also attended the exercise.

THIS STORY IS NOT GOOD FOR ANY MEDIA, MAY BE A MILITARY MAGAZINE WHERE THE READERS ARE INTERESTED IN ALL THESE DETAILS.

HERE I AM REPRODUCING VERBATIM A STORY BY THE IRANIAN NEWS AGENCY IRNA. IT IS A GOOD STORY AND HAS ALL THE FACTS. BUT LOOK HOW LONG THE SENTENCES ARE, AND HOW MANY RULES HAVE BEEN BROKEN. TRY TO READ THIS FOR RADIO. YOU WILL LOSE YOUR BREATH.

Iran appears peeved with India for virtually abandoning the Iran-Pakistan-India (IPI) gas pipeline and joining the proposed Turkmenistan-Afghanistan-Pakistan-India (TAPI) pipeline project, apparently under US pressure.

Addressing a press conference in New Delhi last week on the eve of the 32nd anniversary of the Islamic Revolution, Iranian Ambassador to India Seyed Mehdi Nabizadeh claimed that his country did not look at the IPI project from the narrow perspective of making financial and economic gains.

The project was rather aimed at promoting friendly and cordial relations, particularly between India and Pakistan.

Nabizadeh also noted that both the projects had more or less the same security considerations. He was obviously referring to the fact that both the proposed pipelines would pass through terrorism-affected areas – TAPI through Pakistan and Afghanistan and IPI through Pakistan. New Delhi recently signed an accord to import natural gas through the US-backed TAPI, whose terms are said to be far less stringent than those it had set for pipeline involving Iran.

Replying to a question, the Iranian envoy said Iran had completed 90 percent of the pipeline work inside its territory and only 150 km of the construction activity was to be completed. Similarly, Pakistan had also started the construction work inside its territory. "Under the pipeline project, we will transfer 50 per cent of the gas to Pakistan, while another 50 per cent will be transferred to any other country, like India, willing to join the project," Nabizadeh said.

APPLY THE "BALANCE FACTOR" IN THE FOLLOWING EXAMPLES

According to a global market research firm, India's Tata Nano, billed as the world's cheapest car, has finished bottom of a customer satisfaction survey.

The car just got 70 points on the TNS Global's Customer Satisfaction Survey, while its closest competitor Maruti Alto scored 91.

The survey covered cost-of-ownership, brand image, sales satisfaction, product quality, vehicle performance and after-sales service.

TNS Global says its survey covered almost 9,000 new vehicle owners in 38 cities and spanned 66 models.

"The owners of Tata Nano expect more in terms of design," TNS said.

NOW THIS STORY CANNOT BE COMPLETE UNTIL THE WRITER CAN GET A COMMENT FROM TATA MOTORS TO BALANCE THE STORY. IF HE OR SHE COULDN'T THEN IT HAS TO BE SAID THAT TATA OFFICIALS WERE NOT AVAILABLE FOR COMMENT OR

WHETHER THEY REFUSED TO COMMENT.

Police defused a time bomb planted at a check post in Chingikhel area of Landikotal as one of the three Khassadars, injured in the militant attack on the previous night, died in hospital.

Hospital officials say Ahmed Afridi, personnel of the Khassadar force who had got multiple bullet injuries in the attack, died in Hayatabad Medical Complex. Police say his body has been shifted to Bazaar Zakhakhel for burial.

Four members of the Khassadar Force were killed when militants attacked the newly established check post in Chingikhel area on Pak-Afghan Highway in the tehsil of Landikotal.

THIS STORY IS TOO LOCAL, AND HAS TOO MANY NAMES OF PLACES IN IT. AND IF ONE DOES NOT KNOW THE REGION, HE OR SHE

WILL BE TOTALLY LOST IN SO MUCH DETAIL.

AVOID REPETITION OF WORDS AND NAMES IN THE SAME SENTENCE

***Pakistani** President Asif Ali Zardari and **Kuwait** Amir Shaykh Sabah al-Ahmad al-Jabir al-Sabah have expressed resolve to further strengthen the **relations between Pakistan and Kuwait** through extensive trade cooperation and joint ventures.*

IN THIS LEAD YOU DON'T HAVE TO SAY "RELATIONS BETWEEN PAKISTAN AND KUWAIT"....YOU CAN SAY "RELATIONS BETWEEN THE TWO COUNTRIES" SINCE WE ALREADY HAVE IDENTIFIED THE TWO LEADERS EARLIER IN THE LEAD.

THIS IS LIKE SAYING...THE COW HAS FOUR LEGS. THE COW HAS TWO HORNS.

THE COW HAS ONE TAIL. WE DON'T HAVE TO REPEAT THE WORD COW AGAIN AND AGAIN. WE CAN USE "IT" IN THE SECOND REFERENCE.

BUT IT IS NOT ALWAYS TRUE AND SOME TIMES THERE ARE EXCEPTIONS. FOR EXAMPLE, IN THIS GOOD DOUBLE BARREL LEAD WE HAVE TO REPEAT THE COUNTRY'S NAME TO KEEP IT EASY TO UNDERSTAND.

The U.N. Security Council met urgently on Saturday to consider new sanctions against Libya to halt a violent crackdown on anti-government protesters, but members disagreed over a proposal to refer Libya's leader to an international war crimes tribunal.

EXAMPLE OF TOO MANY ADJECTIVES

A devastating earthquake shook northern India on

Friday. No damage or casualties have been reported. Or a powerful bomb exploded in Karachi, Pakistan killing two people.

PLEASE DON'T USE UNNECESSARY ADJECTIVES AND LET THE CUSTOMER DECIDE HOW DEVASTATING THE QUAKE WAS OR HOW POWERFUL THE BOMB WAS. THE NUMBERS WILL TELL THE STORY. IT IS A TRAP WHEN YOU USE ADJECTIVES BECAUSE IF THE QUAKE WAS "DEVASTATING", THEN WHY NO DAMAGE OR INJURY WAS REPORTED? AND IF THE BOMB WAS "POWERFUL", THEN WHY SO FEW PEOPLE WERE KILLED ?

NOW HERE IS A STORY I WROTE WHERE ADJECTIVES SHOULD BE USED AND ALSO SEEM APPROPRIATE. BUT THE CUSTOMER WOULD LIKE TO KNOW WHAT A "TED

CONFERENCE" IS.

Reports from California say that at an upcoming TED conference, mind-boggling science and undertakings that overwhelm the senses, will inspire the brilliant and accomplished to change the world for the better.

They say artists, celebrities, scientists and technology titans will be among those taking part in the annual event that has changed from an elite gathering into an Internet platform for spreading worthy ideas.

SO WE SHOULD ADD TO THE STORY PRETTY EARLY THAT "TED" IS A NON-PROFIT FOUNDATION DEDICATED TO PROMOTE NEW IDEAS AND INNOVATIONS.

CHAPTER-6

EXAMPLES OF FORMATS FOR A TV STORY

Here I am giving you some examples of how to prepare a TV package. You will need the premise of the story, sound bites from the interviews you did and also appropriate B-roll. Please note the following points in the examples, which have real situations but fictional names of the interviewees except when they are government leaders or officials.

1. Whatever the story is about, it should begin and end with the best footage you have in order to catch the attention of the viewer as you begin telling a story and leave a lasting impression as you end it. In case of the packages on the Afghan war for example, it could be a bomb blast, or a scene of a war. In the case of a story about India-

US relations, it could be a dramatic sound bite about the relations. I guess, every story is different and you will have to figure out how to begin and end and what best shots to use.

2. The sound bites should be short and to the point in order to sustain the attention of the viewer. If you have to have a long bite, cut it into two and write a paragraph in between so that you can narrate it yourself. Or you can paraphrase and narrate the first half of the bite yourself and then introduce the second half of the bite. It should be short and swift. Sometimes, even one-liners can do the trick. For example, in one of my packages I wanted to show a leader to be "dictatorial". So I took one line from her bite in which she says "This is what we have decided to do". It showed what I wanted to and also saved a lot of precious time in a two-minute TV package.

3. Make sure that each sound bite advances the story that in the end completes the premise of your story. In the six examples I am including, you will find the premise of the story in the introduction and then the package that follows would try to prove the premise.

4. Try to use natural sound called NATS in your story to break the monotony. For example when you use crowd scenes, establish the crowd with NATS. When you show violent clashes between police and protesters, establish NATS before you say anything about the demonstration. If you are showing the Taliban or Al-Qaida in action, establish the sound of the fire from their weapons as NATS. When you are showing scenes of an election, establish NATS of campaign etc. I hope you get the drift by now. Think hard and find a way to use NATS. Say if we are going to

show a school, it is common sense to show students playing in the playground or as they leave their classes during recess, because at that time they are making a lot of noise and it will be natural to establish the school with our NATS.

5. Remember, the overall quality of the story depends on your narration and the B-roll. If you have shot the B-roll yourself, then you are limited to what you have unless you can find appropriate shots in the Tape Library. But if all is coming from the Archives, please take time to select the B-roll. Just to remind you that the B-roll is crucial because it is being seen with your narration. So it should never be out of place.

Also remember that if you have shot the B-roll yourself, you can write the story to match the video and if you are using the Archives, you will have to find appropriate footage to match what you wrote. The best way in the second case is to look at the video first and then write your story.

6. NEVER EVER, add background music to your NEWS stories. I have watched several esteemed Indian News channels and seen background music being used with a serious news story. Remember, as soon as you add music with your news story, it becomes FICTION simply because what you are showing on the screen as News is REAL and there was no music being played when you shot the scenes. Adding music simply means the story is not REAL and it has added elements in it and that makes it fiction.

This is a TRAP, that some of the international channels were caught in also. I remember during the first Gulf War, there was an esteemed TV channel that began its coverage with a visual montage of the war scenes with very dramatic music in the background. After several weeks of playing that they came to their senses and eliminated that stupid "introduction" to their coverage. It seemed some executive producer intervened and they began presenting their Gulf War news, simply as NEWS.

7. Always insert the words "FILE" on the screen if the B-roll is not current. Say if you are talking about the Afghan fighting in Kandahar that took place on June 6th but the B-roll is of a fight that took place earlier, do not give the dishonest impression that it took place on June 6th. Say "FILE" on the screen. I have found some reputed American and international TV channels missing the "FILE" part and giving a false impression to the viewer.

8. Remember, when you are using sound bites, some of the names and terms that are in your

narration, may also be pronounced by the people in your sound bites. So listen to the bites beforehand and match the two pronunciations. It should never happen that you pronounce "Hamid' as "Hameeeed" emphasizing the second syllable, and your expert calls him "Hamid" with the emphasis on the first syllable, and correctly so.

9. Note that by dividing the page vertically, you can easily give clues for production on the left side – you can jot down clues for the producer and the tape editor, telling them what B-roll goes over your narration and also you can write time-codes for the bites you chose for the package from your already taped interviews. The text of your narration and the sound bites can appear on the right side. This is a universal format used by almost all TV reporters.

EXAMPLE 1

PRODUCTION CLUES	
	ANCHOR Afghan President Hamid Karzai comes to Washington next week. He comes amid his efforts to reconcile with the Taliban. Our correspondent Ramesh Pandey discussed the visit with some Washington experts, who say some significant differences still persist.
Obama and Karzai in Kabul	REPORTER President Karzai will be looking for support for his efforts to reconcile with some of the senior Taliban leaders.
Set up Jones	But some experts feel the Taliban leadership has no reason to talk at this time. John Jones at the Center for International Affairs.
	JOHN JONES, ANALYST " We should realize that the top of the Taliban have made constant progress at least since 2004. So they have no reason to reconcile or make compromises when they think they are winning."
Set up Weiner	REPORTER Mideast expert John Weiner says he doubts Mr. Karzai is serious when he talks about involving top Taliban leaders.
	JOHN WEINER, MIDEAST ANALYST "We must realize that President Karzai is under international pressure. So his interest in talking to the Taliban is simply a way of distracting people from that pressure. He is

	simply playing the nationalist card and has no serious idea of striking a deal with the Taliban."
	REPORTER
Taliban leaders	Experts also emphasize that the Taliban leadership is not unified. So John Jones says if there is any reconciliation, it will not be at the top, but at the level of provinces and districts. But there are serious differences on that too.
	JOHN JONES, ANALYST
	"There are differences among the U.S. experts, and ISAF experts on Afganistan. The new head of Unama (the UN Mission in Afganistan) is looking at this issue and bringing the United Nations into this for the first time.
	REPORTER
Obama, Karzai	But Jones says when Karzai talks to President Obama, possibly a broad outline of the future strategy will emerge.
	JOHN JONES, ANALYST
	"There will be a host of compromises and agreements which won't be announced. And there will be a list of un-reconciled differences, a few may hit the press, but most are not going to be made public."
	REPORTER
Low level taliban	The Obama administration, so far, has been in favor of urging only the low-level foot soldiers to change sides, and not the top

	leadership.
Kandahar ops	It says the ongoing crackdown on the Taliban in southern Kandahar province could weaken the Taliban over the next six to 12 months.
Set up Rodgers	But Jim Rodgers at the Global Endowment, who just returned from a trip to Afghanistan, disagrees.
	JIM RODGERS, GLOBAL ENDOWMENT "What I have seen there, we cannot break the Taliban insurgency in Kandahar, the city or the province. It is totally out of question."
	REPORTER
Afghan Taliban, I-S-I Chief	But in Kabul the fear is that if Washington waits too long to decide about talking to the Taliban, the Pakistani Intelligence Agency I-S-I will take control, as it did in the 1990s after the Soviet forces withdrew and Washington abandoned Afghanistan.
Pakistani army, Afghan people	And the ground reality is that most Afghans and the regional powers such as India, Iran, Russia and the five Central Asian Republics are totally against any major role for the Pakistani Intelligence in Afghanistan. END

EXAMPLE 2

	ANCHOR This week's International Donors' Conference in Kabul spoke of a 2014 timeline set by President Karzai for an Afghan takeover of its own security from international forces, and also about its decision to channel 50 percent of their foreign aid through the Karzai government. As our Correspondent Radha Sharma reports, prominent analysts say the decisions present both perils and possibilities.
	REPORTER
PRODUCTION CLUES US forces in Kandahar reu footage	As the donors met this week in Kabul, the US-led NATO forces continued their crackdown on the Taliban in Southern Afghanistan – the success or failure of which will determine the future of NATO's latest Afghan strategy.
reu footage	Here, in southern Kandhar province, US troops staged a mortar attack on a Taliban hideout in the Arghandab valley.
Arghandab valley	The valley is a major transit route for Taliban fighters into Kandahar - where they launch quick bombings and retreat.
Wide shots of conference	In Kabul, meanwhile, President Karzai set 2014 as a definite timeline for Afghans to takeover security from the international forces.

	HAMID KARZAI, AFGHAN PRESIDENT
Reuters 7/20	"Our Afghan national security forces will be responsible for all military and law enforcement operations throughout our country by 2014."
	REPORTER
Set up ban ki-moon	UN Secretary General Ban Ki-moon welcomed the deadline, saying the time frame will at last provide Afghans with a chance to decide their own future.
	REPORTER
US troops in Afghanistan	Experts say the Afghan situation presents the United States with a case of contradictory needs. On the one hand, the US has to prove its commitment. But on the other, it must show that it has no intention to be there forever. Burton Smith is a former US ambassador to NATO.
Set up Smith	BURTON SMITH, FORMER NATO ENVOY "The July 2011 date set by President Obama to begin the withdrawal of US troops from Afghanistan is too soon. It gave people the impression that we are just about leaving. So putting something further out in the future as a horizon is important both to show the commitment and also show the desire in the long term to leave after it is successful."
	REPORTER
US troops	Some analysts say President Karzai's timeline also provides a basis for the rest of international community to start scheduling its own troop withdrawal.

British parliament	British Deputy Prime Minister Nick Clegg was the first to talk about it on Wednesday, just one day after the Kabul conference.
Reuters	NICK CLEGG, BRITISH DEPUTY PRIME MINISTER "No timetable could be chiseled in stone, but we are absolutely determined, given how long we've been in Afghanistan – given that we are six months into an 18-month military strategy, we must be out of our combat role by 2015."
Conference, poverty	REPORTER The international donors at the conference also agreed to channel at least half of their aid money directly through the Karzai government, which so far has been tainted by allegations of corruption.
Clinton at the conf.	And Secretary of State Hillary Clinton said for the first time that she was encouraged by Mr. Karzai's efforts to combat corruption in his government.
Jones set up	But analysts like John Jones at International Affairs Center remain skeptical. He says the US and its allies are equally responsible for making the corruption possible for various reasons.
	JOHN JONES "A total lack of control of auditing of the aid money, a lack of focus on effectiveness (of the aid) and Afghan needs, time and again the question is to carry out a plan that suits

	the prejudices and desires of the country that's giving the aid, rather than what the Afghans need."
	REPORTER Observers say the two highlights of the conference should assure the Afghans that the US and its allies are there to empower
Afghan masses in Kabul	Afghanistan – to help Afghans to gradually gain control and eventually manage their own country. END

EXAMPLE 3	
	ANCHOR Washington says the Afghan war is harder than the war in Iraq, so President Obama's troop surge strategy there will take more time to succeed. But a group of Afghanistan experts in Washington say Obama should re-define his strategy to scale back the military operation, and push for a meaningful political reconciliation. Jai Mohan has more on this.
PRODUCTION CLUES US troops in Valley	REPORTER US emphasizes that the offensive here in the Arghandab valley has gone exactly as planned.
	CAPTAIN NICK STOUT, COMPANY COMMANDER "This place has been the key to our success operation for sometime now."
AFP B ROLL	REPORTER So far, there have been no US or Afghan deaths, and US troops now control areas totally new to them. But they acknowledge their frustration, saying the Taliban melted away rather than fight.
AFP B ROLL	So now, the tough job for the troops is winning over a distrustful people who are largely sympathetic to Taliban.
Obama	President Obama acknowledges that the Afghan war is harder than the war in Iraq – and says that key aspects of his troop surge

Wide shot of experts	plan will take time to succeed.
	But a group of experts on Afghanistan says the President needs to rethink his strategy and scale back the military footprints in the country.
US troops Set up Miller	The group known as "Afghanistan Study Group" says the large US presence is having a negative impact, because it is now seen as an occupation force by the locals. And that, it says, has encouraged the Taliban.
Aptn	John Miller is a former CIA analyst
9/11 trade towers	JOHN MILLER, FORMER CIA ANALYST "Our presence there also encourages closer cooperation among extremist groups in Afghanistan and Pakistan."
	REPORTER The group argues there is disconnect between the reason the US went to Afghanistan nine years ago and what it is trying to achieve now.
Bin Laden and al-Qaida fighters	The analysts say the original mission was to permanently destroy Al-Qaida hideouts, and they say most of those have now been destroyed. They also say Al-Qaida is so scattered right now, there is a big question mark about its return.
	Again, John Miller

Set up Shultz	JOHN MILLER, FORMER CIA ANALYST "Even if given the opportunity to return to Afghanistan, it is not at all apparent that Al-Qaida will see an advantage in doing so."
	REPORTER But the members of the group do differ on some points. Author and analyst John Shultz wants the US to ensure that Al-Qaida cannot return.
	JOHN SHULTZ, AUTHOR, ANALYST "I think we should not presume that it will not happen, We must create conditions to make sure that it cannot happen."
Drones, planes, taliban	REPORTER But the group says the US only needs air and naval power and not a large number of ground troops to create those conditions. And it says the military effort should be aimed at achieving reconciliation among the various political groups, including the Taliban.
Karzai (reu)	
karzai	They note that Afghan President Hamid Karzai has appointed a committee to negotiate peace talks with the Taliban.
	PRESIDENT KARZAI (IN DARI) ... Calling for the Taliban to renounce violence and respect the country's constitution.
Taliban	REPORTER But the Taliban so far has rejected any calls

Set up Henry, Taliban	for talks, saying international forces must first leave Afghanistan. Matthew Henry of the New Global Foundation says accepting the constitution should not be a condition for talks. And he says the US should support bringing all kinds of Taliban into the mix. He says the US cannot fight its way to its objective, but can negotiate its way to bring stability and development. MATTHEW HENRY, NEW GLOBAL FOUNDATION "Only a political accord can bring in those groups that are now supporting the Taliban and you will not have stability necessary to achieve anything as long as these groups feel excluded from the government."
US economy, Afghan poverty	REPORTER The study group says the US is spending almost 100 billion dollars a year in Afghanistan, and considering the poor status of the US economy – Obama administration must make sure the benefits of spending that much money are more than the cost. END

EXAMPLE 4

	ANCHOR Afghanistan's Election Commission says it has received hundreds of complaints of fraud about last week's parliamentary elections. But prominent Afghan watchers in Washington say signs of progress in Afghanistan are tied more to security and quality of life than Western style legitimacy in elections. Our Correspondent Karuna Sharma has more from Kabul.
PRODUCTION CLUES	REPORTER More than four million Afghans braved violence and Taliban threats to elect a new parliament. But with final results not expected until the end of October
VOTING crowds	complaints of election fraud are being registered.
KARZAI	President Hamid Karzai is not claiming success. Some even see a level of failure.
Set up SHARIF	Sayeed Morad Sharif is the chairman of the Electoral Complaints Commission.
	SAYEED MORAD SHARIF, E-C-C CHAIRMAN "We have received more than 2,000 formal and written complaints. So far we've looked at some 500 complaints and are taking action about all complaints, God willing."
Complaints being filed	REPORTER Opposition leader Abdullah Abdullah says the vote count is plagued by massive fraud

Afghan masses in Kabul	and urges President Karzai's government to prevent it from happening in the future."
	REPORTER So the question is, after three decades of war, what does "progress" mean in Afghanistan? Afghans do not expect Western style legitimacy in their elections, says John Jones at the Center for International Affairs.
	JOHN JONES "Legitimacy in Afghanistan means better security and better conditions of life and a trustworthy government that can provide services to its citizens."
White house, Capitol Hill	REPORTER And the Afghan election is being closely watched in Washington ahead of a planned strategy review in December, which will likely examine the pace of U.S. troop withdrawals expected to begin in 2011.
General Petraeus	Jones says the election results are not going to impact the December review for which General David Petraeus has laid out several benchmarks.
Kandahar, taliban	They include the elimination of Taliban sanctuaries outside the city of Kandahar, an increase in the number of Taliban fighters brought into a government reintegration scheme, and improvement in the capabilities of Afghan security forces.

	JOHN JONES "If we start setting benchmarks based on our political desires rather than the reality, the conditions on the ground, we almost ensure the Taliban win because they have a strategy of political attrition. They don't win by fighting us, they win by out waiting us."
Set up, petraeus	REPORTER Author Tim Jones is a longtime Afghan watcher. He notes that both General Petraeus and the White House have started downplaying the December strategy review.
	TIM JONES "I think that they want to kind of continue with what they have without anybody saying that it is not working."
Capitol hill, fighting	REPORTER But the observers say patience is a must in the Afghan war, and too much political pressure on the U.S. Army to produce rapid progress will only guarantee a defeat. END

EXAMPLE 5

	ANCHOR India says it is sending a fact-finding mission to its Kashmir region to gather information about the unrest that has left scores of people dead over the last three months. The decision came at a meeting on Wednesday of political leaders in New Delhi. Our Correspondent Ramesh Pandey has more.
PRODUCTION CLUES	REPORTER Clashes between protesters and security forces continued in Kashmir on Wednesday even as leaders from all political parties met in New Delhi to discuss how to resolve the three month old crisis.
Clashes, meeting Clashes	Protests are not new to Kashmir. But these young Kashmiris are not the usual suspects behind the violence that has been a serious problem for the divided region since 1989 when the Muslim separatist movement took a serious turn.
Set up Smith	Peter Smith at Georgetown University.
	PETER SMITH, GEORGETOWN UNIVERSITY "This time the Kashmiri youths are protesting against their quality of life. Many are well educated and unemployed and they feel oppressed by the large presence of military and police."

Set up Anderson	REPORTER John Anderson at American University says another difference is that this time India cannot blame this trouble on its neighbor, Pakistan.
	JOHN ANDERSON, AMERICAN UNIVERSITY "These mobs are homegrown. In the past the Indian argument that much of it was due to cross-border activities could be validated and there may be still certain element of that. But this one seems to be more homegrown."
PM Singh in Kashmir	REPORTER Prime Minister Manmohan Singh also recognized this growing frustration when he promised a huge development package for the region before last general elections. But Peter Smith says the results are yet to come.
	PETER SMITH, GEORGETOWN UNIVERSITY "The benefits of these economic packages have not yet tickled down."
Set up Mirwaiz	REPORTER Mirwaiz Omar Farooq leads Hurriyat, the umbrella group of Kashmir separatists.
	MIRWAIZ OMAR FAROOQ, HURRIYAT CHAIRMAN "We don't want economic packages. We don't want jobs. We don't want incentives. We don't want autonomy. We want freedom."

Kashmir industry	REPORTER And this kind of standoff leads to lack of jobs, says Ajit Bawa, the president of Industrial Association of Kashmir.
Set up Bawa	Ajit Bawa, President, Industrial Association of Kashmir
	AJIT BAWA, PRESIDENT, INDUSTRIAL ASSOCIATION OF KASHMIR "The standoff means less production, less sales and fewer jobs for the Kashmiri youths."
Kashmir demos	REPORTER Kashmiri youth also resent the special powers given to Indian troops in Kashmir for picking up and detaining separatists.
Mirwaiz with supporters	And the Hurriyat umbrella group has made the withdrawal of these powers a precondition for any talks with the government.
Mehbooba and clashes	But another influential leader in Kashmir — the leader of Kashmir's People's Democratic Party, Mehbooba Mufti, says that if the ongoing crisis is viewed from a humanitarian angle, there is no place for any pre-conditions.
	MEHBOOBA MUFTI, CHIEF OF PEOPLE'S DEMOCRATIC PARTY "The Prime Minister must offer an unconditional dialogue, and Hurriyat should also not put forward any condition

	and they should have a dialogue."
	REPORTER
Best shots of clashes	But then she herself put a pre-condition. Before the dialogue, she says, the government must release all jailed demonstrators and end what she describes as a siege of Kashmiri people.
	END

EXAMPLE 6

	ANCHOR "India is an emerging power not just in South Asia but throughout Asia." This is how US President Obama describes India. A joint statement issued after this week's talks between the top leaders of the two countries says Washington welcomes India's leadership role in helping to shape the rise of a stable, peaceful and prosperous Asia. Some analysts caution that in the long run this could bring to the fore the existing rivalry between India and China and determine Asia's future. More on this, in this report by our Correspondent, Ramesh Pandey.
PRODUCTION CLUES	PRESIDENT BARACK OBAMA "India is a leader in Asia and around the world. It's a rising power and a responsible global power."
Obama at washington talks	REPORTER
Obama at talks	President Barack Obama also said relations between the two countries will be a defining partnership in the 21st century.
Set up Smith	This is the first time that the U.S. has described India not just as a power in South Asia but in all of Asia, says Liz Smith, a senior South Asia analyst in Washington.
	LIZ SMITH, ANALYST "I think it is a very important shift in perspective on the U.S. part."

	REPORTER
Washington talks	She says this also impacts the respective relations of the two countries with China, another giant of Asia.
	LIZ SMITH, ANALYST
	"A new scenario is developing in Asia, where India and the United States have a strong interest in seeing that as Asia develops – the whole, large region – develops with a kind of equilibrium among the major players."
	REPORTER
Blake, Singh in Singapore	Assistant Secretary of State Robert Blake agrees and points to India's recent "look-east" policy and its increasing influence in Southeast Asia.
	ROBERT BLAKE, ASSISTANT SECRETARY OF STATE
	"The conversation has been quite serious about how the United States and India can work more together in Asia."
	REPORTER
Singh at asean meeting, Rosen	But India's increasing influence in Asia coupled with its new strategic partnership with the United States may prove irksome for China, says Frank Rosen of the Howard University.
	FRANK ROSEN, HOWARD UNIVERSITY
–	"As India's role in Asia increases, China might want to remind India that China really is the boss in the region and any time

	it wants to beat up India, it can."
	REPORTER
Map of south asia graphics	And Lisa Fellini of the Global Strategy Group says China is doing so already by making significant inroads in the South Asian countries surrounding India.
	LISA FELLINI, ANALYST "China is contributing to the port infrastructure in Gwadar in Pakistan, and in Sri Lanka. And now the Indians are also facing a Chinese facility in a port in Bangladesh armed with Chinese supplied anti-ship missiles."
	REPORTER
Zardari in Beijing	China's close military relations with Pakistan are already a concern for India, she says.
Tibet, Dalai Lama	And Frank Rosen says China is concerned about India's strategy in Tibet and its support to Tibet's spiritual leader, the Dalai Lama.
	FRANK ROSEN, ANALYST "The level of unrest in Tibet may go up and the Indian government may not simply walk away, saying whatever China does is acceptable to us."
	REPORTER
Indian & chinese leaders	Experts say although it is apparent that India and China are trying to improve their economic and trade relations, no one can

	ignore that both are vying for dominance in Asia.
Montage of Obama, singh, singh with chinese leaders and obama in china	They say what is to be carefully watched in Asia in the near future is the relations between India and China, and also their respective relations with the United States. END

Reference page 67

Disclosure scheme for foreign assets soon

WIN-WIN To cover NRIs too; lower taxes, legal immunity on offer

Debobrat Ghose
debobrataghose@hindustantimes.com

NEW DELHI: The government is working out the details of a voluntary income disclosure scheme that would offer a window for bringing back undisclosed assets stashed away in overseas tax havens into the country's financial system.

The Offshore Voluntary Compliance Scheme will cover Indian organisations, citizens and non-resident Indians (NRIs), and offer immunity from criminal prosecution and imprisonment, besides lower rates of interest and penalties.

Also, the authorities will not insist on disclosure of the source of money once it is done voluntarily. But in case the tax department tracks down undisclosed assets through its networks, the holder of the money would face "strong punitive actions, including high penalties, prosecution and even imprisonment", said a government source.

The last such offer — the Voluntary Disclosure of Income Scheme (VDIS), introduced in 1997 to fight internal black money generation — was an unconventional, but successful one. More than 350,000 people disclosed their income and assets under the scheme that brought in ₹7,800 crore. The scheme was closed on December 31, 1998.

An expert group of the Central Board of Direct Taxes (CBDT), assigned by the government to curb the generation and transfer of black money abroad and bring the funds back, recommended the new scheme.

The source said, "It ... modeled on the ... Offshore Volu... Initiative run ... Revenue Servi... US."

Under attack by civil society and social activist Anna Hazare for alleged inaction over money stashed away in foreign accounts, the governmen... posed an action pla... amendment o... other ... com... ank-tanks ... ational Institute ... Finance and Policy, ...ational Institute of Financial Management and the National Council for Applied Economic Research — has been set up to estima... he quantum of black mo... rated in India.

...erim recommen... P task force esti... amount generated ... Independence at $500 billion (about ₹22.5 lakh crore) to $1.4 trillion (about ₹63 lakh crore).

A recent study by Global Financial Integrity, a Washington-based research group, estimated the current value of illicit money outflow from India at $462 billion (about ₹20.79 lakh crore).

A FRESH BAIT

- The Offshore Voluntary Compliance Scheme will offer Indian organisations and citizens, including NRIs, the chance to pay taxes on slush funds parked in foreign bank accounts
- It will be modeled on the lines of Offshore Voluntary Disclosure Initiative run by the US Internal Revenue Service
- The last such offer — Voluntary Disclosure of Income Scheme — was launched in 1997
- An expert group of the Central Board of Direct Taxes recommended the scheme
- Govt commissioned a study by think-tanks NIPFP, NIFM and NCAER to estimate the size of India's black economy

INDIA'S BLACK MONEY ESTIMATE

A BJP task force estimated the amount at $500 billion (about **₹22.5 lakh crore**) to $1.4 trillion (about **₹63 lakh crore**)

Global Financial Integrity, a Washington-based research group, estimated the present value of illicit money outflow from India at $462 billion (**₹20.79 lakh crore**)

Wisdom Village Publications Pvt Ltd

Knowledge is information. Wisdom is transformation.

Some Other Books by WISDOM VILLAGE PUBLICATIONS Pvt Ltd

Broom & Groom
MRP Rs 195/-
Kiran Bedi
Pavan Choudary

Art of Getting People To say yes
MRP 200/-
Arvinder Brara

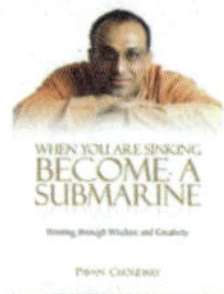

When you are Sinking become a Submarine
MRP Rs 195/-
Pavan Choudary

Pavan Choudary

Chanakya's Political Wisdom
MPR Rs 100/-(HB)

Confucius' Social Wisdom
MPR Rs 100/-(HB)

Kabir's Spiritual Wisdom
MPR Rs 100/-(HB)

Success Sutras for the 21st Century
Set of 3 Books(HardBound) in a Box
MRP Rs 290/-

Healing in your Hands
(Acupressure)
MRP Rs 250/-
Dr. Anand Verma

The Rx Factor
(Pharmaceutical Marketing-Reprint)
MRP Rs 125/-
Pavan Choudary

Arise Awake
MRP Rs 225/-
Dr. P.V. Vaidyanathan

Setbacks to Comebacks
MRP Rs 150/-
Nishit Lal

ORDER YOUR COPY. ON BULK ORDERS AVAIL SPECIAL DISCOUNT
CONTACT -+91 98108 00469, wvpdindia@gmail.com